DANIEL'S PROPHECY OF THE 70 WEEKS

DANIEL'S PROPHECY OF THE 70 WEEKS

DR. ALVA J. McCLAIN

ZONDERVAN
PUBLISHING HOUSE
OF THE ZONDERVAN CORPORATION | GRAND RAPIDS, MICHIGAN 49506

DANIEL'S PROPHECY OF THE SEVENTY WEEKS
Copyright 1940, 1969, by
Alva J. McClain

Published by
Zondervan Publishing House
Grand Rapids, Michigan

*The Bible text used is the King James Version, with some
changes taken from the American Standard Version of 1901,
copyright, 1929, by the International Council of Religious
Education, and used by permission.*

Twenty-eighth printing 1981
ISBN 0-310-29012-0

Printed in the United States of America

*About the Time of the End, a body of
men will be raised up who will turn
their attention to the Prophecies, and
insist upon their literal interpretation,
in the midst of much clamor and oppo-
sition.* —SIR ISAAC NEWTON

CONTENTS

Foreword 7

Introduction 9

PART I

The First Sixty-nine Weeks and the Coming
of the Messianic Prince 17

PART II

The Parenthesis of Time Between the Sixty-ninth
and Seventieth Weeks 31

PART III

The Seventieth Week and The Coming of the
Roman Prince 49

Chart . . . . 68 and 69

Appendix 71

FOREWORD

The "seventy weeks" refers to the prophecy in Daniel 9:24-27 which, in contrast to the general prophecies in Daniel 2 and 7, pin-points the time within the fourth kingdom when the Messiah shall appear. Bible scholars are generally agreed that the "weeks" designate "weeks of years" (490 years).

In clear, lucid style, Dr. Alva J. McClain examines *Daniel's Prophecy of the 70 Weeks* and expounds this important Scriptural passage in a scholarly, in-depth study. In his words, "A proper understanding of the seventy weeks of Daniel not only safeguards the Christian against the elaborate guess-work of those who persist in setting dates for the Lord's return, but also furnishes the infallible key to the real chronology of all New Testament prophecy."

Moody Monthly, in reviewing this book, said of it: "It is a pleasure to recommend this book to those who are seeking to understand this prophecy. It clearly brings to light in a succinct way the essential truths contained in this prophecy."

Dr. Alva J. McClain, Th.M., D.D., was for 25 years President of Grace Theological Seminary in Winona Lake, Indiana, and is regarded as one of the outstanding Bible scholars of his generation. It is a pleasure to make a new edition of his book available to a new generation of Bible scholars and prophetic students.

THE PUBLISHERS

INTRODUCTION

THE very brief but famous prophecy of the Seventy Weeks, recorded in Daniel 9:24-27, has always been a focus of interest to interpreters of the Word, regardless of their theological bias. But today more than ever, in the face of significant tendencies both in the world and the professing church, the passage is attracting fresh attention, especially from those who still believe in the reality of "predictive prophecy." Probably no single prophetic utterance is more crucial in the fields of Biblical Interpretation, Apologetics, and Eschatology.

In the first place, the prophecy of the Seventy Weeks has *an immense evidential value as a witness to the truth of Scripture*. That part of the prophecy relating to the first sixty-nine weeks has already been accurately fulfilled (as I expect to show), and in this remarkable fulfillment we have an unanswerable argument for the divine inspiration of the Bible. It is, in fact, nothing less than a mathematical demonstration. For only an omniscient God could have foretold over five hundred years in advance the very day on which the Messiah would ride into Jerusalem and present Himself as the "Prince" of Israel. Yet this is precisely what has been done in the prophecy of the Seventy Weeks.

Again, this great prophecy is *the impregnable rock upon which all naturalistic theories of prophecy are shattered*. These theories deny the possibility of any "predictive element" in prophecy. And since the Book of Daniel did forecast many well attested historic events, the critics have sought to save their theories by denying to Daniel the authorship of the book and moving its date down to a point subsequent to the events described, thus making the unknown author a mere historian who pretended to be a prophet. In this rather easy and summary fashion, they hoped to get rid of the troublesome specter of "predictive prophecy." But no critic has ever dared to suggest a date for the Book of Daniel as late as the birth of our Lord. Yet Daniel's prophecy of the Seventy Weeks predicts to the very day Christ's appearance as the "Prince" of Israel. Therefore, when the critics have done their worst, no matter where they place the date of the book, the greatest time-prophecy of the Bible is left untouched. And on this prophecy, the whole case of the critics goes to pieces. For if even so much as *one* predictive prophecy is established, there remains no valid a priori reason for denying the others.

Finally, with reference to its importance, I am convinced that in the predictions of the Seventy Weeks, we have *the indispensable chronological key to all New Testament prophecy*. Our Lord's great prophetical discourse recorded in Matthew and Mark fixes the time of Israel's final and greatest trouble definitely within the days of the Seventieth Week of Daniel's prophecy (Dan. 9:27; Matt. 24: 15-22; Mark 13:14-20). And the greater part of the Book of Revelation is simply an expansion of Daniel's prophecy within the chronological framework as outlined by the same Seventieth Week, which is divided into two equal periods, each extending for 1260 days, or 42 months, or 3½ years

(Rev. 11:2-3; 12:6, 14; 13:5). Therefore, apart from an understanding of the details of the Seventy Weeks of Daniel, all attempts to interpret New Testament prophecy must fail in large measure. This point will be discussed fully in Parts II and III.

The prophecy of the Seventy Weeks was given to Daniel under circumstances which were most remarkable. Daniel and his people had been carried away captive into the land of Babylon. The armies of Nebuchadnezzar had utterly desolated the city of Jerusalem (2 Chron. 36:17-21). According to an earlier prophecy uttered by Jeremiah, these "desolations" were to last for a period of seventy years (Jer. 25:11). The ninth chapter of Daniel opens with a reference to this very prophecy (9:1-2). The prophet Daniel, now a man grown old in the service and courts of the Babylonian kings, understands from his study of the "Books" that the period of divine judgment must be nearing its close; and he prays to the God of Israel for light as to the future of his "city" and his "people" (9:3-19). It is a marvelous prayer, but unfinished; for while the petitioner "was speaking in prayer" an angelic messenger came with the answer of God (21-23). And since the divine reply contains a prediction of the First Advent of Christ, it is wholly appropriate that the messenger should have been Gabriel, the same angel who several hundred years later would announce His birth of the Virgin Mary (Luke 1:26). Thus it was the angel, not Daniel, who first uttered the great prophecy of the Seventy Weeks. The passage appears as follows in the Common Version, with the exception of a few changes selected from the American Standard Revised Version and indicated by brackets:

11

24. Seventy weeks are determined upon thy people and upon thy holy city, to finish the transgression, and to make an end of sins, and to make reconciliation for iniquity, and to bring in everlasting righteousness, and to seal up the vision and prophecy, and to anoint the most Holy.

25. Know therefore and understand, that from the going forth of the commandment to restore and to build Jerusalem unto the Messiah the Prince shall be seven weeks, and threescore and two weeks: the street shall be built again, and the wall, even in troublous times.

26. And after [the] threescore and two weeks shall Messiah be cut off, [and shall have nothing]: and the people of the prince that shall come shall destroy the city and the sanctuary; and the end thereof shall be with a flood, [and even unto the end shall be war]; desolations are determined.

27. And he shall [make a firm covenant] with many for one week: and in the midst of the week he shall cause the sacrifice and the oblation to cease; [and upon the wing of abominations shall come one that maketh desolate; and even unto the full end, and that determined, shall wrath be poured out upon the desolate].

With the prophecy now before us, we shall begin the study with a careful analysis of its main features. Because of their importance, and as an aid to the interpretation of the passage, the reader should note carefully and keep in mind the following points:

1. The entire prophecy has to do with Daniel's "people" and Daniel's "city," that is, the nation of *Israel* and the city of *Jerusalem* (24).

2. Two different princes are mentioned, who should not be confused: the first is named *Messiah the Prince* (25); and the second is described as *Prince that shall come* (26).

12

3. The entire time-period involved is exactly specified as *Seventy Weeks* (24); and these Seventy Weeks are further divided into three lesser periods: first, a period of *seven weeks;* after that a period of *three-score and two weeks;* and finally, a period of *one week* (25, 27).

4. The beginning of the whole period of the Seventy Weeks is definitely fixed at "*the going forth of the commandment to restore and to build Jerusalem*" (25).

5. The end of the *seven weeks and threescore and two weeks* (69 weeks) will be marked by the *appearance of Messiah as the "Prince" of Israel* (25).

6. At a later time, "after the threescore and two weeks" which follow the first seven weeks (that is, after 69 weeks), *Messiah the Prince will be "cut off,"* and *Jerusalem will again be destroyed* by the people of another "prince" who is yet to come (26).

7. After these two important events, we come to the last, or Seventieth Week, the beginning of which will be clearly marked by the establishment of a *firm covenant* or treaty between the Coming Prince and the Jewish nation for a period of "one week" (27).

8. In the "midst" of this Seventieth Week, evidently breaking his treaty, the Coming Prince will suddenly *cause the Jewish sacrifice to cease* and precipitate upon this people a time of wrath and desolation lasting to the "full end" of the Week (27).

9. With the full completion of the whole period of the Seventy Weeks, there will be ushered in *a time of great and unparalleled blessings for the nation of Israel* (24).

PART I

THE FIRST SIXTY-NINE WEEKS AND THE
COMING OF THE MESSIANIC PRINCE

In approaching the first sixty-nine weeks of the prophecy, it should be remembered that this period of sixty-nine weeks begins with the "going forth of the commandment to restore and to build Jerusalem" and that it ends with the manifestation of Messiah as the "Prince" of Israel. Our purpose will be to ascertain the nature and length of the "weeks," discover in history the events which mark their beginning and end, and then see whether the prediction fits the history from a chronological standpoint; for the one point in the prophecy upon which all interpreters agree is that the first sixty-nine weeks have been fulfilled and are past. About four questions will cover the field of investigation.

I. What Is the Measure of Time Indicated by the "Weeks" of this Prophecy?

What kind of "weeks" are they? To the casual English reader, the word "week" means but one thing, that is, a period of seven *days*. And many interpreters have accepted this rather superficial view of the matter. Taking the "Seventy Weeks" as "weeks" of days, they have then proceeded to translate the days into *years*. If we ask by what

17

right they take such liberties with the inspired Word of God, they answer that "in prophecy a day stands for a year." This is the so-called "Year-Day" theory of prophetic interpretation employed by certain Protestant writers and also by Seventh Day Adventism and Russellism. To me it has always seemed an arbitrary method, although claiming the support of some great names. I cannot discover any sound Biblical authority for putting "years" where the sacred text reads "days." The folly of this system appears most clearly in attempts to handle the 1260 days of Revelation 12:6, which constitute simply one-half of the Seventieth Week of Daniel's prophecy. Here the "Year-Day" theorists are compelled either to abandon their scheme or else make *one-half* of the last week of Daniel equal to over twice as many years as are found in the other sixty-nine and one-half weeks. The precise figures, according to this theory, would be as follows: 69½ weeks equal 486½ years; but the last ½ week equals 1260 years! If such a violent and inconsistent device is the only way, as some have claimed, to make the prophecy "come out right," then we had better cease all attempts to interpret prophecy. It is this sort of thing that makes the skeptics smile and brings the whole study of prophecy into disrepute.

Turning now to the simple facts concerning these "weeks" in Daniel, we shall find no necessity for tampering with the exact language of the text. The Hebrew word is *shabua*, which means literally a "seven," and it would be well to read the passage thus, dropping for a moment the word "week" which to the English ear always means a week of days. Thus the twenty-fourth verse of Daniel's ninth chapter simply asserts that "seventy *sevens* are determined" (cf. Stuart's translation), and what these "sevens" are must be determined from the context and from other Scriptures. The evidence is quite clear and sufficient, as follows:

Most important is the fact that in their divinely inspired calendar, the Jews had a "seven" of *years* as well as a "seven" of *days*. And this Biblical "week" of years was just as familiar to the Jew as the "week" of days. It was, in certain respects, even more important. *Six years* the Jew was free to till and sow his land, but the *seventh year* was to be a solemn "Sabbath of rest unto the land" (Lev. 25: 3-4). Upon a multiple of this important week of years — "seven Sabbaths of years" — there was based the great jubilee of social and economic adjustment every fiftieth year, when debts were wiped out, estates returned to the original holders, and slaves went free (Lev. 25:8-9). Nothing could be so important to the Jew as this week of years.

Now there are several reasons for believing that the "Seventy Sevens" of Daniel's prophecy refer to this well known "*seven*" of years. In the first place, the prophet Daniel had been thinking not only in terms of years rather than days, but also in a definite multiple of "sevens" (10 x 7) of years (Dan. 9:1-2). Second, Daniel also knew that the very length of the Babylonian captivity had been based on Jewish violations of the divine law of the Sabbatic year. Since according to 2 Chronicles 36:21 the Jews had been removed from off the land in order that it might rest for *seventy* years, it should be evident that the Sabbatic year had been violated for 490 years, or exactly seventy "sevens" of years. How appropriate, therefore, that now at the end of the judgment for these violations the angel should be sent to reveal the start of a *new era* of God's dealing with the Jew which would extend for the same number of years covered by his violations of the Sabbatic year, namely, a cycle of 490 years, or "Seventy Sevens" of years (Dan. 9:24).

Furthermore, the whole context of the prophecy demands that the "Seventy Sevens" be understood in terms of years. For if we make them "sevens" of days, the entire period would extend for merely 490 days or a little over *one* year. Considering now that within this brief space of time the city is to be re-built and once more destroyed (to say nothing of the tremendous events of verse 24), it becomes clear that such an interpretation is altogether improbable and untenable. Finally, there is a remarkable and convincing argument based on the usage of the Hebrew word, curiously overlooked by many of the commentators. Outside of the prophecy of the "Seventy Weeks," the Hebrew word *shabua* is found only in one other passage of the book (10:2-3), where the prophet states that he mourned and fasted "three full *weeks*." Now, here it is perfectly obvious that the context demands "weeks" of *days*, for Daniel would hardly have fasted twenty-one years! And significantly, the Hebrew here reads literally "three sevens *of days*." Now, if in the ninth chapter, the writer intended us to understand that the "Seventy Sevens" are composed of days, why did he not use the same form of expression adopted in chapter ten? The quite obvious answer is that Daniel used the Hebrew *shabua* alone when referring to the well known "week" of years, a customary usage which every Jew would understand; but in chapter ten, when he speaks of the "three weeks" of fasting, he definitely specifies them as "weeks of *days*" in order to distinguish them from the "weeks" of *years* in chapter nine. And if the "weeks" of chapter nine were composed of days, there would have been no possible reason for changing the Hebrew form in chapter ten.

Therefore, by every fair and sensible rule of interpretation, the "Seventy Sevens" must be understood as years, not days which we must surreptitiously change into years to make the prophecy come out right.

II. IF THESE "WEEKS" ARE COMPOSED OF YEARS, WHAT IS THE LENGTH OF THE YEAR?

It is quite well known that the various calendars of the nations have used years of different lengths, correcting the error by the addition of days from time to time. Even our own year of 365 days is not exact, the shortage being a little less than one day in four years. If, therefore, the time of the Seventy Weeks is to be calculated exactly, we must know the length of the year involved. And unless this information is supplied by the inspired Word, the case is hopeless. But there is conclusive evidence to show that the prophetic year of Scripture is composed of 360 days, or twelve months of 30 days.

The first argument is *historical*. According to the Genesis record, the Flood began on the seventeenth day of the second month (7:11), and came to an end on the seventeenth day of the seventh month (8:4). Now, this is a period of exactly five months, and fortunately the length of the same period is given in terms of days — "an hundred and fifty days" (7:24; 8:3). Thus the earliest known month used in Biblical history was evidently thirty days in length, and twelve such months would give us a 360-day year.

The second argument is *prophetical* and is absolutely conclusive because it is based on a measure included within the prophecy of the Seventy Weeks under discussion. Daniel 9:27 mentions a period of Jewish persecution at the hands of the Coming Prince who will make a covenant with that people. Since this persecution begins in the "midst" of the Seventieth Week and continues to the "end" of the Week, the period is obviously three and one-half years. Daniel 7:24-25 speaks of the same Roman Prince and the same persecution, fixing the duration as "a time and times and the dividing of time" — in the Aramaic,[1] three and a half times. Revelation 13:4-7 speaks of the same great political Ruler and his persecution of the Jewish "saints" lasting "forty and two months." Revelation 12:13-14 refers to the same persecution, stating the duration in the exact terms of Daniel 7:25 as "a time and times and half a time"; and this period is further defined in Revelation 12:6 as "a thousand two hundred and three score days." Thus we have the same period of time variously stated as 3½ years, 42 months, or 1260 days. Therefore, it is clear that the length of the year in the Seventy Weeks prophecy is fixed by Scripture itself as exactly 360 days.[2]

III. WHEN DID THE WHOLE PERIOD OF THE SEVENTY WEEKS BEGIN?

Having found that the Seventy Weeks are "weeks" of *years*, and that these years are each *360* days in length, our next problem is to find the his-

---

[1] See Appendix.
[2] See Appendix.

torical date when the whole period began. And here we are not left in any doubt, for the twenty-fifth verse of the prophecy names a definite historical event: "Know therefore and understand, that from the going forth of *the commandment* to restore and to build Jerusalem unto the Messiah the Prince shall be seven weeks, and threescore and two weeks." If now we can locate this "commandment," or decree, and fix its date accurately, we shall have the terminus from which the prophecy takes its start.

This "commandment," by a large number of interpreters, has been identified with the decrees issued by Cyrus, Darius, and Artaxerxes, recorded in the Book of Ezra. But these decrees without any exception have to do with the rebuilding of the *Temple*, not the city. Let the student read carefully Ezra 1:1-2; 4:1-5, 11-24; 6:1-5, 14-15; 7:11, 20, 27, and notice that in every case the decree concerns the "house of the Lord." But there is no authorization for the rebuilding of the city. And it is an interesting fact that the rebuilding of the Temple was stopped for a time because of accusations from Jewish enemies that the Jews were attempting without authority also to rebuild the *city* (Ezra 4:1-24). The very evident motive on the part of some interpreters to find the decree in Ezra was to get the prophecy of the Weeks started early enough to make the first 69 Weeks end near the *birth* of Christ. Otherwise it is very doubtful whether anyone would ever have turned to the decrees in Ezra. The early date is not only unnecessary but plunges the entire chronology into endless confusion and disagreement.

There is only one decree in Old Testament history which, apart from all expedients of interpretation, can by any possibility be identified as the "commandment" referred to in Daniel's prophecy. That decree is found in the Book of Nehemiah.[3] Let the student read carefully 1:1-4 and 2:1-8, noting several facts: First, that it was a report of the ruined condition of the "wall" and "gates" of the *city* that aroused the deep concern of Nehemiah, Jewish "cupbearer" to King Artaxerxes. Second, that after earnest prayer he dared to petition the King "that thou wouldst send me unto Judah, unto the *city* of my fathers' sepulchres, *that I may build it*" (2:5). Third, that his bold request by the grace of God succeeded, as he tells us: "And the king *granted me*, according to the good hand of my God upon me" (2:8). But most important of all, we should notice how carefully Nehemiah, writing by divine inspiration, records the exact date of this decree: "*in the month Nisan, in the twentieth year of Artaxerxes the king*" (2:1).

For those who believe in Biblical inspiration and the genuineness of predictive prophecy, it will be no surprise to learn that the date fixed by Nehemiah happens to be one of the best known dates in ancient history. Even the *Encyclopaedia Britannica*, certainly not biased in favor of prophecy, sets the date of Artaxerxes' accession as 465 B.C.; and therefore his twentieth year would be 445 B.C.[4] The month was Nisan, and, since no day is given, according to Jewish custom the date would be understood as the first. Hence in our calendar the date would be *March 14, 445* B.C. Here we have the beginning of the Seventy Weeks.

---

[3] See Appendix.
[4] See Appendix.

IV. WHEN DID THE FIRST SIXTY-NINE WEEKS END AND WHAT HAPPENED ON THAT DATE?

Having found that the Weeks are composed of years, that the length of the prophetic year is 360 days, and that these years began on March 14, 445 B.C., the ground is now cleared for the chronological computation. And for this I am indebted to the painstaking research of the late Sir Robert Anderson, the results of which are set forth in his great book, *The Coming Prince*, a work occasionally sneered at by the critics but never answered.

In order to find the *end* of the Sixty-nine Weeks, we must first reduce them to days. Since we have 69 Weeks of seven years each, and each year has 360 days, the equation is as follows: $69 \times 7 \times 360 = 173,880$ *days.* Beginning with March 14, 445 B.C., this number of days brings us to April 6, 32 A.D.

To prove that the 173,880 days equal exactly the period from March 14, 445 B.C., to April 6, 32 A.D., it is necessary to compute this period in terms of our own calendar year, as follows:

445 B.C. to 32 A.D. is 476 years (B.C. 1 to A.D. 1 is one year)

476 x 365 days	173,740 days	
Add for leap-years	116 days	(3 less in four centuries)*
March 14 to April 6	24 days	(inclusive)

Total 173,880 days

April 6, 32 A.D., therefore, is fixed definitely as the end of the era of the first 69 Weeks; and accord-

---

* Note: To divide 476 by 4 would give 119 leap-years. But since century-years are not leap-years unless divisible by 400 and since 476 years involve four centuries, it follows that only one of the four century-years would be a true leap-year. Therefore, it is necessary to subtract 3 from 119 to get the exact number of extra leap-year days in 476 years.

ing to Daniel's prophecy, it should mark the very day of Messiah's manifestation as the *Prince* of Israel. Without attempting to enter into the clear but intricate chronological calculations set forth by Anderson in his book, *The Coming Prince* (pages 95-105), I shall simply state his conclusion that April 6, 32 A.D., was the tenth of Nisan, that momentous day on which our Lord, in fulfillment of Messianic prophecy, rode up to Jerusalem on the "foal of an ass" and offered Himself as the *Prince* and *King* of Israel.

That our Lord understood perfectly the crucial nature of His action on that day is unmistakably clear from the record in Luke 19:28-44, a passage which should be studied carefully noting the following details: First, realizing that the day had arrived for Him to ride up to Jerusalem in fulfillment of Zechariah 9:9, He sends His disciples to procure the "colt" upon which as the *King* He must appear (30-34). Second, the whole multitude of the disciples, clearly understanding the meaning of His act, began to shout a well known quotation from a Messianic Psalm (118:22-26), saying, "Blessed be the *King* that cometh in the name of the Lord" (37-38). Third, although previously He had forbidden the disciples to make Him known as the Messiah, now He rebukes the Pharisees' protest and commends the disciples' shout, saying that "if these should hold their peace, the stones would immediately cry out" (39-40). Certainly something was happening here that had never happened before.

But most important of all, we have from the lips of Christ Himself an estimate of the unparalleled importance of that day and what He was doing. Weeping over the city because He knew in advance the certainty of His rejection, He laments, "If thou hadst known, even thou, in *this thy day*, the *things which belong unto thy peace*, but now they are hid from thine eyes" (42). What "day"? Why, the day God had fixed in Daniel's prophecy, the day that belonged to Israel, the day on which their "Messiah" would manifest Himself as the "Prince," the exact *173,880th* day of the prophecy! And what were "the things" belonging to their peace? They are the identical "things" named in verse 24 of the prophecy of the Seventy Weeks, those marvelous blessings promised to Israel by that God Who never breaks a covenant. But now for a time all these "things" are to be hid from the eyes of the nation; their enemies will prevail over them; and the city will be once more destroyed. But why? The answer is tragic but just: *"Because thou knewest not* THE TIME OF THY VISITATION" (44).

Thus the 173,880 days of the first Sixty-nine Weeks ran their course to the very day — deep and abiding encouragement to all who love the Lord and His precious Word of prophecy.[5] And I close this discussion with but one remark: The exact fulfillment of this prophecy is sufficient to demonstrate the accuracy of Daniel and also by implication the inspiration of the Bible and the truth of Christianity. Only *God* can "declare the end from the beginning" and forecast to the very day "things that are not yet done" (Isa. 46:10).

---

[5] See Appendix.

PART II

THE PARENTHESIS OF TIME BETWEEN
THE SIXTY-NINTH AND
SEVENTIETH WEEKS

THE results of our investigation thus far may be summarized briefly as follows: First, the "weeks" of the prophecy are weeks of years, not days. Second, the length of each of these prophetic years is 360 days. Third, the entire period of "weeks" began with the "commandment" to rebuild Jerusalem, which was issued by Artaxerxes on March 14, 445 B.C. (Neh. 2:1-8). Fourth, from this date to the appearance of Messiah as the "Prince" of Israel was exactly 69 weeks of years, or 483 years (Dan. 9:25). Fifth, at the end of these 69 weeks of years, to the very day, April 6, 32 A.D., our Lord Jesus Christ rode up to Jerusalem on the "foal of an ass" in fulfillment of the well-known prediction of Zechariah (9:9). Thus we have in past history a complete demonstration of the chronological exactness of Daniel's prophecy up to the Seventieth Week.

We now turn our attention to this final "week" of the prophecy. And here the first point to be determined is the exact chronological relation of the Seventieth Week to the Sixty-nine Weeks which precede it. On this question expositors have split into two absolutely distinct schools of interpretation, so radically different that the results reach far into the field of New Testament eschatology. The one school holds to what I shall call the *Continuous* interpretation, and the other to the *Gap* interpretation.

According to the *Continuous* view, the whole period of the Seventy Weeks is continuous and unbroken. There is no break anywhere. The Seventieth Week follows the Sixty-ninth without any gap in time. Obviously, if this theory be correct, the Seventieth Week is past, having come to an end somewhere early in the Book of Acts. Adherents to the theory are not wholly agreed as to details, but the most important group believe that Christ died in the middle of the Seventieth Week and therefore this last Week must have ended three and one-half years after the cross. One curious interpretation takes the 1260 days of the last half of the Seventieth Week, changes these days into years, and thus prolongs the period for 1260 years! But without taking such unwarranted liberties with the Word of God, there is no way for adherents to the Continuous interpretation to prolong the Seventieth Week beyond seven years after the death of Christ, or about 39 A.D. Regardless of minor differences, therefore, it should be clear that according to the Continuous view the whole prophecy of the Seventy Weeks has been fulfilled for over nineteen hundred years, and the future contains nothing comprehended within the scope of the prophecy.

On the other hand, according to what I have called the Gap interpretation, the Seventieth Week does not immediately follow the Sixty-ninth Week, but there is a great parenthesis of time between these two which has already lasted for over nineteen hundred years, and therefore the Seventieth

Week still lies in the future. At first sight, to those not familiar with certain characteristics of Messianic prophecy, this will seem a very startling view. And some have earnestly denounced it as a violent expedient of interpretation. What right, they ask, do we have to sunder this final week from the first sixty-nine and arbitrarily push it nineteen centuries into the future? How can such a method be justified? In reply, we must admit immediately that the objectors are wholly within their rights in demanding some good reasons for this method of interpretation. And unless such reasons can be given, we should not expect men to accept it. But there are plenty of convincing reasons. In fact, the deeper one pushes into the prophetic Word, the greater in number and importance do these evidences appear.

1. *Such a gap in time before the Seventieth Week is implied by the most natural reading of the prophecy.*

This seems so clear to me today that it is hard to understand how along with many others I could have missed the point so long. But doubtless, like the average English reader, I came to the passage with what the late Dr. M. G. Kyle liked to call "our Anglo-Saxon passion for a continuous chronology," a thing in which the Oriental mind was not greatly interested. And it is quite possible that no one would ever have thought of making the last "one week" continuous with the first Sixty-nine Weeks had it not been for the language of verse 24, where we read that "seventy weeks are determined." And having read this expression — *Seventy Weeks* — we at once jumped to the conclusion that all seventy were continuous and then carried this erroneous impression throughout the reading of the rest of the prophecy.

But let the student now read carefully the analysis of the "weeks" in verses 25-27 forgetting, if possible, the expression of verse 24, and notice the order of events. First, in verse 25 we have a period of Sixty-nine Weeks ending with a definite historical event, the appearance of Messiah the Prince. Then, *after* these Sixty-nine Weeks* come two other events, the death of Messiah and the destruction of the city. And after these two events, we come to the final *one week* in verse 27. If we follow the order of the record strictly, both the death of Messiah and the destruction of Jerusalem are placed between the Sixty-ninth and Seventieth Weeks of prophecy. This leads directly to a second important argument:

2. *A gap in time between the Sixty-ninth and Seventieth Weeks is demanded by the historical fulfilment of the two predicted events of verse 26.*

These events were the death of Messiah and the destruction of Jerusalem, and both of them are placed *after*, not within, the Sixty-nine Weeks. Now, it is a well-known fact of history that in the year 70 A.D., Titus, the Roman, destroyed the city of Jerusalem and its sanctuary in one of the most frightful sieges of all time. And since it is certain that the first Sixty-nine Weeks came to an end not later than 32 A.D., the destruction of the city took

---

* Note: It is not "after threescore and two weeks" but "after the threescore and two weeks" that Messiah is "cut off." That is, He is cut off after "the" Sixty-two Weeks which follow the first "seven weeks," or after a total of Sixty-nine Weeks. Omission of the definite article in the Authorized Version has obscured the meaning. Obviously, however, Messiah could not be cut off seven weeks before He appeared!

34

place nearly *forty* years "after" the close of the Sixty-nine Weeks. Yet in the record of the prophecy, the destruction of the city is placed *before* the last week. Therefore, the very historical fulfillment of this one detail of the prophecy, upon which practically all are agreed, demands a gap of at least thirty-eight years, and thus provides an infallible clue to the problem which has puzzled so many interpreters. For if even so much as one year is allowed between the last two weeks, the *principle* of the "gap interpretation" is admitted. And if, as we have seen, there must be at least thirty-eight years, we have no a priori reason for denying that there may be nineteen hundred. This argument is based squarely on the rock of prophecy *already fulfilled*, than which there is no safer guide as to what we may expect from prophecy which is yet unfulfilled.

3. *The fulfillment of the tremendous events in verse 24 cannot be found anywhere in known history.*

Notice again what they are: "to finish the transgression" — "to make an end of sins" — "to make reconciliation for iniquity" — "to bring in everlasting righteousness" — "to seal up the vision and prophecy" — "to anoint a most holy place" (A.R.V. margin). And, remember two further things: first, all these great events have to do with the *Jewish* people; and, second, they are included within the reach of the Seventy Weeks' prophecy.

Now, if the whole Seventy Weeks are continuous, then, as we have already seen, the Seventieth Week must have ended not later than seven years after the crucifixion, or somewhere early in the Book of Acts.

35

But the history of those years contains nothing that in any reasonable way corresponds with what Daniel saw at the end of the Seventy Weeks. Even if we should adopt the "spiritualizing" scheme of interpretation, still the bed is too short and the cover too narrow. Where in the history of Acts, for example, can you find any finishing of Jewish transgression or an ending of Jewish sins? On the contrary, the transgression of the chosen nation increases by leaps and bounds until the crisis comes in the twenty-eighth chapter, where the Apostle Paul turns definitely to the Gentiles. Or where in the period of the Acts can we find any "sealing up of vision and prophecy"? On the contrary, it is during this very period and beyond that we find the greatest loosing of "vision and prophecy" in all the history of revelation. But at the second coming of our Lord in glory, which will take place at the close of the Seventieth Week, vision and prophecy will no longer be needed. The Word of God Himself will be present in visible manifestation, and His law will go forth from Jerusalem.

4. *An unseen gap in prophetic time is not at all an unusual phenomenon in Old Testament prophecy.*

There are many instances outside of Daniel. The great Messianic prophecy of Isaiah 9:6 is an interesting example. *"For unto us a Child is born"* — the whole Christian world rejoices in the knowledge that this prophecy was fulfilled nineteen centuries ago. But read the next clause: *"And the government shall be upon his shoulder."* Here we have something still future. Between these two clauses of the same prophecy, separated only by a colon in the

English translation, there is a break in time which has already extended nineteen hundred years. There is another excellent example in Zechariah 9:9-10. The Messianic King is presented riding up to His city *"upon a colt the foal of an ass."* All believers know that this is fulfilled and past. Yet the next verse, without the slightest indication of any literary or chronological break, reads on: *"And . . . he shall speak peace unto the heathen,* and his dominion shall be from sea even to sea." Some day this will be done just as literally as the first. But between the two predictions there is the same great parenthesis of time.

One more example must suffice, attested by our Lord Himself. In Isaiah 61:1-2 there is a prophecy which reads as follows: "The Spirit of the Lord God is upon me; because the Lord hath anointed me to preach good tidings unto the meek; he hath sent me to bind up the brokenhearted, to proclaim liberty to the captives, and the opening of the prison to them that are bound; To proclaim the acceptable year of the Lord, and the day of vengeance of our God." Our Lord Jesus must have been deeply interested in this great prophecy concerning Himself, for one day He came to Nazareth and stood up to read from this very passage in the synagogue. But rather strangely, when He had finished the clause, *"To proclaim the acceptable year of the Lord,"* He closed the book and said, "This day is this Scripture fulfilled in your ears" (Luke 4:16-21). Now, the amazing thing is that *He stopped at a comma* (in the English Version). Why did He stop squarely in the middle of a sentence? The answer is that the next following clause, *"And the day of vengeance of our God,"* was not to be fulfilled for over nineteen hundred

years and is still future. By this one single act of
His, our Lord as the infallible Interpreter laid down
the principle of the "gap interpretation," apart from
which the chronology of Old Testament prophecy
is an insoluable enigma.

As a matter of fact, it is well known that there
is often little or no time perspective in the visions of
the Old Testament prophet. He saw events together
on the screen of prophecy which in their fulfillment
were often separated by centuries of time. This
curious characteristic, so strange to Western minds,
was in complete harmony with the Oriental mind,
which was little concerned with a *continuous* chronology. As the late Dr. M. G. Kyle used to tell his
students, the Oriental was interested in the *next*
important event, not in the time which might inter-
vene. And the Bible is an Oriental book, humanly
speaking. However, we do find the prophets themselves perplexed by this lack of time perspective.
Peter tells us that after the prophets had written,
they actually sat down and searched their own writ-
ings to find their meaning: "Searching *what*, or
what manner of time the Spirit of Christ which was
in them did signify, when it testified beforehand the
sufferings of Christ, and the glory that should follow" (1 Peter 1:11). Evidently the prophets saw
clearly both the *sufferings* and *glories* of Christ.
Furthermore, they had the *order* right — first, the
sufferings; after that, the glories. But the one thing
which was not clear to them was the *time* element
— "what, or what manner of time."

Now, this is precisely the problem in the prophecy of the Seventy Weeks. Daniel saw clearly the
sufferings of Christ — Messiah is to be "cut off"
after the Sixty-ninth Week but before the Seventieth

Week. It is equally certain that Daniel saw also the *glories* of Christ — they are to be ushered in at the close of the Seventieth Week (9:24). But it seems quite evident that the intervening time problem was beyond the prophet's understanding, for this very problem is discussed briefly in 12:6-7 by the two angelic messengers, and Daniel confesses, "*I heard but I understood not*" (8). That this failure to understand was not due to any lack of spiritual discernment in the Prophet, but rather to the sovereign plan of God, is clear from the words of verse 9: "Go thy way, Daniel: for the words are closed up and *sealed till the time of the end*." This particular ultimatum does not apply to the entire Book of Daniel, as it is sometimes taught, but only to the time element surrounding the Seventieth Week of the prophecy. The "*time* of the end" will arrive with the beginning of the Seventieth Week, and then prophetic chronology will instantly become so crystal clear that only the "wicked" can possibly misunderstand (12:10). But until the Seventieth Week begins, all attempts to fix prophetic dates must be only so much misspent labor. This point will be discussed more fully later.

5. *As the final argument in favor of the Gap interpretation, I offer the testimony of our Lord Himself to show that the Seventieth Week is still future.*

Verse 27 of the prophecy contains a most peculiar expression: "Upon the wing of abominations shall come one that maketh desolate." The Hebrew is confessedly difficult. Luther rendered it, "Upon the wings stands the *abomination of desolation*." The same general expression occurs also in Daniel

12:11: "the *abomination that maketh desolate*." Without attempting here to fix its precise meaning, the thing we should notice is that Daniel connects it with the stopping of the daily sacrifice, which takes place in the middle of the Seventieth Week. Let the reader keep this fact clearly in mind and turn to Matthew, chapter 24, where our Lord refers to the same thing. In verse 15, He warns His Jewish hearers to flee from their houses to the mountains, "When ye shall see the *abomination of desolation, spoken of by Daniel the prophet*, stand in the holy place." The reason for this warning is indicated in verse 21: "For *then* shall be great tribulation." But they are not to be utterly disheartened, for "*immediately* after the tribulation of those days . . . they shall see *the Son of Man coming* in the clouds of heaven with power and great glory" (29-30).

Now, the argument is very simple and clear: Whatever the "abomination of desolation" may be, there can be no doubt that Daniel put it exactly in the middle of the Seventieth Week, while our Lord placed it at "the end," just before His second coming in glory. Therefore, *the Seventieth Week must also come at the end of the present age just prior to Christ's coming in glory*. This is the interpretation of Christ Himself, and it should settle the matter. Our Lord has not yet come in glory; the Seventieth Week is still future; and there is a great parenthesis of time between the Sixty-ninth and Seventieth Weeks of the prophecy. Thus far we are on solid ground.

If we see clearly and accept the existence of this great parenthesis of unreckoned time between the Sixty-ninth and Seventieth Weeks, and understand that the Seventieth Week is still future, we shall be effectively guarded against some of the dangers which constantly beset the interpreter of prophecy.

First, we shall be kept from the confusion and despair which are so common even among devout scholars when they come to the Seventieth Week and attempt to unravel the chronology of events beyond the First Advent of our Lord. The late Dr. Nathaniel West has well summed up the situation: "The effort to connect it (the Seventieth Week) immediately with the Sixty-ninth has led to results in exegesis both amazing and amusing. Never was the hopelessness of any task more thoroughly evinced than here." The great Hengstenberg insisted upon a literal fulfillment of the Seventy Weeks, yet when he comes to the last one, he confesses that "their terminal point is a vanishing one." Stanley Leathes frankly admits in his reply to the critical Kuenen: "Chronology fails as to the last Week." And Pusey says, "We have not the chronological data to fix it." So completely did many of the greatest Biblical scholars lose their way in utter disagreement that Bosanquet rightly observed: "Every fresh interpretation only adds to the force of our conviction that *some radical error* lies at the foundation of all our Christian interpretations, and, till it is discovered, the Seventy Weeks of Daniel will remain unexplained and inexplicable to the comprehension of every unprejudiced inquirer." This "radical error" was the failure to see the great interval of time between the Sixty-ninth and Seventieth Weeks. Delitzsch stated clearly the general principle which was needed by the interpreters when he said, "All prophecy is complex; that is, it *sees together what history outrolls as separate:* and all prophecy is apotelesmatic; that is, it sees close behind the

41

nearest-coming, epoch-making turn in history, the summit of the End." But along with the others, Delitzsch failed to apply this true principle to the Seventieth Week.

Second, this important principle of interpretation explains why the whole of our present age, so great in many respects, is passed over by the prophets with comparative silence. And it constantly keeps us on our guard against attempting to find things in Old Testament prophecy which are not there. I need not rehearse here the extravagant fancies into which men have been led by their failure to see and apply the principle of the Prophetic Parenthesis, thus often bringing the study of prophecy into disrepute.

In the third place, if we see this principle and understand that the Seventieth Week lies in the future, we shall be saved from that popular but pernicious fallacy which assumes that God is finished with the nation of Israel. "Seventy Weeks are determined upon *thy* people," said the angel to Daniel, and if the last week is yet future, there is still a place for Israel in the divine plan. In fact, the whole plan will be consummated in that final week. And the error of putting the Seventieth Week in immediate connection with the Sixty-ninth has undoubtedly made no small contribution to the erroneous theories of both Post-millennialism and Amillennialism.

Fourth, the acceptance of the Gap interpretation of the Seventieth Week *makes utterly impossible all date-setting schemes* for the present age and for the second coming of our Lord, since the entire parenthesis of time between the Sixty-ninth and Seventieth Weeks is both unrevealed and elastic from the human standpoint. Every scheme of date-setting requires for its basis a continuous prophetic chronology covering the present age. Without this, the date-setters are helpless. And according to the Gap principle, there can be no such chronology. Only an omniscient God could have given such a continuous chronology, and He for good and wise reasons did not give it. Therefore, we need not waste any time even discussing the possibility of setting a date for the Lord's return. It simply cannot be done. And I, for one, am glad that this is so. The Blessed Hope that the Lord may return for His church *at any moment* would be destroyed if the date-setters should ever succeed. But there is no danger. Once the last week of Daniel begins its course, it will be posible for the "wise" to set some accurate dates. But the church will have been taken up at that time.

In concluding this discussion, one more question should be considered. Does the prophecy of Daniel shed any light at all upon the nature of our present age which lies between the Sixty-ninth and Seventieth Weeks? The material is scarce but very significant. The rather amazing thing is that in all this vast chasm of over nineteen centuries, Daniel identifies clearly only two events: the death of Messiah and the destruction of Jerusalem. Outside and beyond these two events, he mentions nothing. All the pomp and glory and boasted achievements of the so-called Christian era are passed over with complete silence. There is something very humbling about this silence, if we have eyes to see. "He that glorieth, let him glory in the Lord."

But if the prophet mentions specifically only two events, he does not altogether ignore the general character of the age. Sweeping through our centuries of "progress" with the eye of divine inspiration, he sums up the whole period in two statements, very startling for their ominous brevity. The first is: *"Unto the end shall be war."* And the second is: *"Desolations are determined"* (see verse 26, A.R.V.). The first statement seems to declare the abysmal failure of unregenerate man apart from God, while the second affirms the decree of a sovereign God to permit the failure and use it for His own wise and holy ends. From these two statements, we may learn some valuable lessons.

In the first place, there will be war on earth among men until the Lord returns. Of course, there are some modern prophets who think otherwise, but we shall do well to stick by Daniel in these matters. As a prophet, he has an *established* reputation. Over two thousand years ago Daniel said that "unto the end shall be war," and no one can deny the accuracy of his prediction *thus far*. Any prophet who has been right for two thousand years is worth listening to. Let the other prophets establish their reputations before asking us to follow their prognostications. Of course, Daniel's prophecy does not mean that all efforts against war in the present age are futile. It is a matter of common knowledge that *some* threatened wars have been stopped in the past, and doubtless others in the future can be stopped. Such efforts are worthwhile. But the point is, no matter how successful the nations may be in avoiding a war here and there, we are to remember that *no permanent peace* can come to this sinful world till the Prince of Peace comes down to earth again in glory. "Unto the end shall be war." We may not like the prophecy; it may humble our rebellious pride; but God hath spoken.

The other lesson is still more important! *The God of heaven is in control* over the events of this sinful age of ours. If war continues to the end, bringing destruction and desolations, we are not to forget that these "desolations are *determined*." Man is responsible for his failure, but man's failure never takes God by surprise. What man does, God has determined. The present age, even at its worst, is not running out of control. An infinite God sits upon the throne of Providence, and He always has the last word in human history. And through all the mystery and confusion of human failure, the great providential formula holds good: "Ye meant evil . . . but God meant it for good" (Gen. 50:20, A.R.V.).

PART III

THE SEVENTIETH WEEK, AND THE
COMING OF THE ROMAN PRINCE

IN PART I of this exposition, it was shown that
the first Sixty-nine of the Seventy Weeks of prophetic years began on March 14, 445 B.C., with the
issuing of King Artaxerxes' decree to rebuild Jerusalem (Neh. 2:1-8); and that the period ended on
April 6, 32 A.D., when our Lord rode up to Jerusalem on the foal of an ass presenting Himself as
the King of Israel (Luke 19:28-44) exactly 69
sevens of years (483) to the very day. In Part II,
it was established that the Seventieth Week did not
follow the Sixty-ninth immediately, but that between the Sixty-ninth and the Seventieth Weeks
there is a vast gap of uncharted time which has
already extended over nineteen hundred years, and
therefore the Seventieth Week of years is still in the
future. Coming now to an investigation of this Seventieth Week and its events, it will be necessary to
reproduce only the last two verses of the prophecy,
which as before are given as they appear in the
King James version with the exception of a few
changes taken from the American Standard Revised
version and indicated by brackets:

26. And after [the] threescore and two weeks shall
Messiah be cut off, [and shall have nothing]: and the

people of the prince that shall come shall destroy the city and the sanctuary; and the end thereof shall be with a flood, [and even unto the end shall be war]; desolations are determined.

27. And he shall [make a firm covenant] with many for one week: and in the midst of the week he shall cause the sacrifice and the oblation to cease; [and upon the wing of abominations shall come one that maketh desolate; and even unto the full end, and that determined, shall wrath be poured out upon the desolate].

Now, the reader should notice carefully that in these verses of the prophecy there are two different princes mentioned: first, "*Messiah the Prince*"; and second, "*the prince that shall come.*" The expression "prince that shall come" cannot possibly refer to "Messiah, the Prince" for the simple reason that it is "the *people* of the prince that shall come" who are to destroy Jerusalem after the death of Messiah. And since it is now a matter of history that Jerusalem was destroyed in A.D. 70 by the *Roman* people, not by the Jewish people, it follows that "the prince that shall come" cannot be the Jewish Messiah but is some great prince who will arise out of the Roman Empire.

Furthermore, we need not speculate about the identity of this coming Roman prince. He is the well-known "little horn" of the seventh chapter of Daniel, with "eyes like the eyes of a man, and a mouth speaking great things," the king "more stout than his fellows," who rises swiftly among the ten kings of the Revived Roman Empire of the end-time, and who for a brief season shall wield almost unlimited power over the nations of the world. His well-known identity is undoubtedly one reason why in chapter nine he is referred to simply as "the prince that shall come." For those who had read the great vision of chapter seven, no further identification would be needed. This same prince is, in my judgment, also the "king of fierce [strong] countenance" of chapter eight, the Wilful King of chapter eleven, the "man of sin" of 2 Thessalonians 2:3, the beast "out of the sea" of Revelation 13:1; the last great persecutor of Israel, Satan's false Christ,* before whom all the world shall do homage whose names are not written in the Lamb's book of life. A dark and sinister figure he is, whose ominous shadow falls constantly upon the pages of divine prophecy, until he comes to his fearful doom in the lake of fire (Rev. 20:20).

Turning now to verse 27 of the prophecy of the Weeks, which deals specifically with the Seventieth Week, our first problem is to identify the antecedent of the pronoun "*he*," for this person is the chief actor and subject of the verse. Does the "he" refer back to the Messianic prince or to the Roman prince? Grammatically, it might refer to either, although presumption favors the latter because he is mentioned last before the pronoun. However, there are certain other considerations which are decisive. First, we are told that "*he*" will make a firm covenant with the Jewish nation for a period of one week, or seven years. Now, there is absolutely nothing recorded in the earthly ministry of our Lord which even remotely resembles such a covenant. Those who hold that Messiah is the maker of this

---

* Note: Some feel that the coming prince of Dan. 9:27 cannot also be the personal Antichrist, because the first is a Roman while the latter (they argue) must be a Jew. This, however, is no serious problem, for the same person could be a Roman *politically* and at the same time a Jew *racially*.

seven-year covenant have never been able to produce the evidence to show the existence of such a covenant between our Lord and the Jews. They cannot point to the place in history where it began nor where it has ended. Second, the theory that this covenant was made by our Lord when He began His earthly ministry and that by His death He caused the Jewish sacrifice to cease, breaks down because there is no reference to such a covenant in the Gospel records and also because the death of Christ did not cause the Jewish sacrifices to cease. They continued, in fact, until the destruction of Jerusalem nearly forty years later. And, since according to this theory Christ died "in the midst of the week," the sacrifices should have ceased immediately. But they did not. In the third place, to insist that Messiah was the maker of this seven-year covenant necessarily puts the entire Seventieth Week in the *past*, immediately following the Sixty-ninth Week. But this is impossible, as we have seen already from arguments set forth in Part II. The Seventieth Week is still in the future, not in the past, according to the Word of our Lord Himself in the twenty-fourth chapter of Matthew.

The maker of the "firm covenant" described in Daniel 9:27 cannot be "Messiah the prince." His covenants with His chosen people are everlasting, not limited to a period of seven years. The one who makes the seven-year covenant is the Roman Prince, the one "that shall come." It is he, not the Lord Jesus Christ, who is the subject of verse 27 and the chief actor in the terrible events of its seven-year period. (So Godet, Hofmann, Tregelles, and others.) We are ready now to consider the Seventieth and last week of the prophecy.

1. *This Seventieth Week is a period of seven years which lies prophetically between the translation of the church and the return of Christ in glory.*

We have already seen that this Seventieth Week of years must still be future for various reasons which need not be rehearsed here, but particularly because our Lord Himself places the "abomination of desolation" of the Seventieth Week at the end of the present age just prior to His return in power and glory (Matt. 24:15-30). But now, examining more closely its exact location in relation to the events of the end-time, we shall find that the Seventieth Week cannot begin to run its course in fulfillment of the prophecy until the true church has been taken out of the world by translation. Keeping in mind that Daniel's prophecy pictures the Seventieth Week as the definite period of the revelation and career of this terrible Roman prince, let us turn to 2 Thessalonians 2:1-9 where the Apostle Paul discusses his revelation in relation to the career of the true church upon the earth. Verses 6-8 read as follows in the American Standard Version: "And now ye know *that which restraineth* to the end that he may be revealed in his own season. For the mystery of lawlessness doth already work; only there is *one that restraineth* now, until he be taken out of the way. And *then* shall be revealed the Lawless One, whom the Lord Jesus shall slay with the breath of His mouth, and bring to nought by the manifestation of his coming."

Now, since the restraining power mentioned in this remarkable passage can be nothing else but the *true church indwelt by the Holy Spirit*, it is clear that the coming Roman prince cannot be revealed as the "man of sin" as long as this restraining power is operative on earth. But when this "one that restraineth" shall be "taken out of the way" (as the church shall be taken one of these days, according to 1 Thessalonians 4:13-18), "*then* shall be revealed the lawless one." The language is unmistakable and indicates two important facts: first, the coming prince cannot be revealed until *after* the removal of the true church from the earth; and, second, his revelation must follow the translation of the church very speedily, if not immediately. Therefore, since the identity of the Roman prince will be clearly revealed the moment he makes his seven-year covenant with the Jewish people, and since the making of this covenant will mark the beginning of the Seventieth Week, it follows logically that the Seventieth Week cannot begin until after the removal of the true church from the earth.

It is also certain that this Seventieth Week must come to an end at the return of our Lord from heaven in glory, for the following reasons: First, Daniel 9:24 names certain great blessings which will come to Israel when the whole period of the Seventy Weeks have run their course, and a study of these blessings shows that they are the very ones which are to be brought by Messiah at His second coming from heaven in great power and glory. Second, since the awful power of the Roman prince continues to the full end of the Seventieth Week (Dan. 7:25-27; 9:27), and since he is to be "destroyed" by the manifestation of our Lord's coming (2 Thess. 2:8), it follows that this glorious coming of our Lord will take place at the end of the Seventieth Week. In fact, it will be the glorious second coming of Messiah which will terminate the entire period of the Seventy Weeks and usher in the covenanted blessings to Israel.

2. *This Seventieth Week also provides the exact chronological framework for the great events recorded in chapters six to nineteen of the Book of Revelation.*

It is a fact, open to all who can read, that the only chronological data of these chapters are in every case based upon a single measure of time which is variously stated as "a time, and times, and a half a time" (12:14), "forty and two months" (11:2; 13:5), and "a thousand two hundred and threescore days" (11:3; 12:6). Now, disregarding for a moment all the finespun theories about the meaning of these phrases, and sticking to the common-sense meaning of words, it is evident that we have here just one measure of time, that is, exactly *three and a half prophetic years of 360 days each.*

These are the simple facts. But what have interpreters done with them? There are, roughly speaking, three schools of opinion. One school regards all prophetic numbers as merely symbolic and therefore meaningless from the standpoint of chronology. A second school, holding to the unscriptural "year-day" theory of prophetic interpretation, has proceeded to erect all kinds of fantastic chronological schemes covering the present age, even to the extent of setting dates for the coming of the Lord. A third school, noting that the three and a half years of Revelation are exactly one-half of seven years, and remembering that Daniel's prophecy divides the Seventieth Week into two halves, has used Daniel's prophecy of the Seventy Weeks as a point of departure and the inspired key to the interpretation of the

Book of Revelation, which was the obvious and sensible thing to do.

There is one question, however: Since the chronology in the Book of Revelation is always stated in terms of *one-half* of seven years, do the events of the book cover only one-half of the Seventieth Week or can both halves of the week be identified? I believe that the entire Seventieth Week of seven years can be located in the Book of Revelation, and that the key passage is 11:2-3, which reads as follows: "But the court which is without the temple leave out, and measure it not; for it is given unto the Gentiles [nations]: and the holy city shall they tread under foot *forty and two months*. And I will give power unto my two witnesses; and they shall prophesy a *thousand two hundred and threescore days*, clothed in sackcloth."

Now, since the *"forty and two months"* of verse 2 constitute a three and a half year period during which Gentile powers shall "tread under foot" the Holy City, this must refer to the *last half* of Daniel's Seventieth Week, because it is in the middle of the Seventieth Week that the Roman prince stops the Jewish sacrifice and becomes their persecutor (Dan. 9:27). It is likewise apparent that the *"thousand two hundred and threescore days"* of verse 3 must refer to the *first half* of the Seventieth Week, because the two witnesses bear their testimony during this period, and they cannot be slain until the Roman beast comes to the height of his power when it is "given unto him to make war with the saints, and to *overcome* them" (Rev. 11:7; 13:7). Thus we have here clearly the entire Seventieth Week: the first half as the period of the rising power of the Roman prince and the testimony of the Two Witnesses; while the second half is the period of the Beast's absolute dominion over the world and his terrible persecution of Israel. The exact middle of the Seventieth Week is marked by the killing of the Witnesses and the sounding of the "seventh angel" (Rev. 11:1-15).

Only one question remains: Can we locate the beginning and the end of this Seventieth Week in the record of the Book of Revelation? Since we already know that the week will end with the glorious appearing of the true Christ from heaven, it is clear that the seven-year period must *end* in chapter 19, verses 11 to 21. And since the period begins with the revelation of the false Christ, as we have seen above, the Seventieth Week must *begin* in Revelation 6:1-2, where the Roman beast begins his ruthless ride to world power. Thus chapters six to nineteen of Revelation cover the Seventieth Week of Daniel's prophecy, an exact period of seven prophetic years divided into two equal halves at the sounding of the "seventh angel." Borne along by the same Spirit of prophecy, Daniel furnishes the chronological frame and John fills in the details. If we separate the two, prophecy becomes an insoluble enigma.

3. *The Seventieth Week will begin with the making of a "firm covenant" between the coming Roman prince and the Jewish people.*

The exact language of the prophecy is, "He shall make a firm covenant with [the] many for one week" (9:27). It has been affirmed by some that the Hebrew *Berith* used here cannot mean a "covenant" between men but must refer to a covenant on the part of *God*. They overlook the fact, however,

57

that the same Hebrew term is used of the treaty made between Ahab and Benhadad (1 Kings 20: 34), of the treaty between Ephraim and Assyria (Hos. 12:1), and also of the treaty between Antiochus and Ptolemy Philometer (Dan. 11:22). The same Hebrew word is translated fifteen times in the Old Testament by our English word "league."

The precise nature of this "firm covenant," league, or treaty, between the Roman prince and the Jewish people is not revealed fully in Daniel 9:27. But there is at least an intimation in the verse. The fact that, following the establishment of the treaty, the Roman prince only three and one-half years later puts a stop to the Jewish sacrifices, certainly suggests that one thing involved in the treaty will be the reestablishment of the Jewish Temple sacrificial system.

Now this fits accurately into the present historical situation and dilemma of the Jew today.[6] In the midst of all the great Jewish activity in the Land of Palestine just now there still remains one heartbreaking problem. Regardless of material and cultural progress, and it is very great, the Jew can never be satisfied until his ancient Temple is restored and the Mosaic ritual reestablished. But on the very spot where this Temple must be built, there now stands a Mohammendan mosque, one of the most sacred places in the world to millions of Moslem people. And so the United Nations finds itself today in a most unenviable position, trying to satisfy the conflicting ambitions in Palestine of two irreconcilable parties — the Jew and the Moslem — and being denounced by both sides.

---

[6] See Appendix.

What is left today of an agonizing Jewry is demanding political protection for the development of their age-long dream of a national home in Palestine. The question is, Where can the Jew find such protection? The United States is interested, but would hardly agree to assume the sole responsibility. Russia, of course, would be only too glad to take over in that land which is the gateway to three continents, the very "navel" of the earth, as the prophet Ezekiel names it. But such an arrangement would conflict violently with other interests. There remains another possible solution, namely, the commission of the problem to a *group* of powers. If the countries should agree to such a solution, it would doubtless have to be a group with interests centering in the Mediterranean area, a group opposed to Russian Communism, and yet not strong enough to dispute the supremacy of other nations in this area.

Now it is precisely in this area that the final Roman prince of Daniel 9:27 will effect his ten-horn coalition, beginning his own mad career as a "little horn" politically (Dan. 7:8). Yet in the brief space of three and one-half years he must rise to the pinnacle of world domination. Such an amazing achievement is not impossible, but it will require vast munitions of warfare. To get them he will need two things — political prestige and financial support. Thus the present historical situation contains some of the motives for the treaty predicted by Daniel. The Jew wants protection in Palestine and is willing to pay for it. Many of the Mediterranean nations are desperately poor. England and America are unalterably opposed to Russian control there. The Roman Catholic Vatican, in the name of religion, is calling for a holy war against Communism.

The British government has found it impossible politically for her to do for the Jews in Palestine what was promised under the Balfour agreement. In the complex of this situation, what an opportunity for the rise of the "little horn"! He could declare his hatred for Red Communism, offer to become the champion of religion in general and the Vatican in particular, secure financial aid from the Jews by promising to sponsor their aspirations in the Holy Land, and probably receive the moral backing of the civilized world. Such a combination of forces would be almost incalcuable. Some day a Roman[7] "prince" will do something of this kind, and the event may be nearer than we think. Science has created a new and strange environment in which history can move with incredible speed. And the world's bewilderment is filled with Satanic opportunity.

4. *In the middle of the Seventieth Week, the Roman prince will suddenly reverse his friendly attitude toward the Jews and "cause the sacrifice and the oblation to cease."*

Quite evidently, after the seven-year treaty has run for only three and one-half years, the Roman prince tears up his agreement as a mere scrap of paper. In this violent and faithless procedure, he manifests the spirit of present-day trends, which are already distressingly clear. There was a time when nations had some regard for their solemn agreements, but covenant-breaking seems to have become the fashion of the age. Mr. C. J. Hambro, a distinguished statesman and journalist of Norway, has said: "No state believes wholeheartedly in any

---

[7] See Appendix.

promise given by other states today. Covenants, pacts, treaties, conventions, and agreements violated on the slightest pretext, and obligations, undertakings, promises, and guarantees unfulfilled, have left the world in a state of moral chaos. As states have gone off gold, so they have gone off their whole system of political responsibilities." It is not a pleasant picture. We live today in a world of what is called "power politics," which means that force has taken the place of morality. And let us not forget that when he arrives, the Roman beast will honor only a "god of forces" (Dan. 11:38).

But what are the motives which lead the Roman prince to tear up his treaty with the Jewish people? The reasons for his change of attitude are not stated in the prophecy of the Seventy Weeks. But one reason may be deduced easily from what we know of his character and career. No one could hate our Lord Jesus Christ and at the same time really love the chosen people from which He came according to the flesh. By his very nature, the Man of Sin will be violently anti-Semitic. His treaty with the Jews will be based wholly on political expediency. Therefore, once he has reached the pinnacle of world power aided by their great wealth and influence, he will have no further use for them. Like certain rulers today, he keeps his treaties only as long as it is profitable to do so. And as he will break with the Jewish people in the middle of the Seventieth Week, even so he will break with the apostate church which he has supported as long as he needed her influence in his rise to world power. Just as the Jew will pay dearly for the treaty with the Roman beast, so the great harlot will pay dearly for her ride (Rev. 17:16).

But there is another reason for the Roman prince's change of attitude toward the Jew. From 2 Thessalonians 2:4 and Revelation 13:8-15 we learn that, intoxicated with his great power, he will actually take his seat in the temple of God and demand the honors and worship of God Himself. This to the sternly monotheistic Jew will certainly be the very "abomination of desolation," and many will refuse to bow the knee, in spite of the fact that this idolatrous worship will become almost universal (Rev. 13:8). This refusal on the part of godly Jews will furnish the Roman beast with the necessary pretext for the breaking of his treaty and the forcible cessation of the Jewish Temple sacrifice. It should be noted here that according to the exact language of Daniel 9:27, the beast's treaty will be made with *the many* of the Jewish nation, the clear implication being that *some* Jews will not join in the compact from the beginning of the last week. Furthermore, we should not forget the effect of the testimony of the Two Witnesses, who undoubtedly will denounce the treaty throughout their ministry during the first half of the week and seal their testimony with martyrdom.

To some, this idea of the modern world worshiping a *man* may seem to be utterly incredible. But already there are certain tendencies appearing in the world of scholarship and religion which are leading definitely in this direction. First, there is the popular doctrine of the "finite God." Second, there is the identification of this "God" with the "soul," or "social consciousness," of humanity. And third, there is a growing recognition of the high value of symbolism in religion. These tendencies finally can lead to but one end: Let the world once come to identify God with humanity, and the next logical step will be the apotheosis of some great representative of humanity as a symbol of God. And the coming prince will be the greatest man (save One) the world has ever seen. For that matter, men have always been able to find reasons for worshiping themselves. F. L. Godet, noted Swiss theologian, pointed out that the "theological system" of the Antichrist could be summed up in three propositions: "1. There is no personal God without and above the universe. 2. Man is himself his own god — the god of this world. 3. I am the representative of humanity; by worshiping me, humanity worships itself." More than ever in our day we may see the rapid development of this humanistic religion, which will reach its consummation in the blasphemous claims of the Roman beast. But, thank God, even in his awful day, there will be some who will refuse to bow the knee.

5. *The breaking of the "firm covenant" between the Jews and the Roman prince will mark the beginning of a period of unparalleled "desolations" for the Jewish people.*

Since this period of "desolations" begins in the middle of the last week and lasts "even unto the full end" (9:27), obviously it will continue for three and a half years. This is exactly the time specified in Daniel 7:25 during which the Roman beast "shall wear out the saints of the Most High"; the same measure of time given in Revelation 13: 5-7 when this beast "shall make war with the saints and . . . overcome them"; the same time mentioned in Revelation 11:2, during which the holy city shall be trodden down of the Gentile nations; the same time referred to in Revelation 12:6, 14, during which the "woman" (Israel) shall be given the special protection of God. Thus all of divine prophecy fits together perfectly: The same persecutor, the same kind of persecution, the same nation under persecution, and exactly the same length of time. A number of very ingenious prophetic schemes have been worked out by the artifice of taking these 1260 days and turning them into years. How much more simple and satisfactory it is to take these passages just as they read without any tampering with the language. In this way, the prophecy of the Book of Revelation synchronizes exactly with Daniel's great prophecy of the end-time.

This is the "time of Jacob's trouble" (Jer. 30:7) so fully discussed by the Old Testament prophets. As a divinely inspired prediction, it was an old story in the days of Daniel. Daniel's contribution to the prophecy was to provide the chronology of the period of persecution. Our Lord paid special attention to this period in the future history of Israel, warning them solemnly that "when ye therefore shall see the *abomination of desolation*, spoken of by Daniel the prophet, stand in the holy place. . . . Then let them which be in Judea flee into the mountains . . . for *then* shall be great tribulation, such as was not since the beginning of the world to this time, no, nor ever shall be" (Matt. 24:15-21). It should be noticed that our Lord sets the beginning of this terrible persecution at the time of the placing of the "abomination of desolation" in the "holy place," which can be nothing else but that moment in the middle of the week when the beast breaks his treaty, stops the sacrifice, and usurps for himself the holy place of divine worship in the Temple.

The outbreak and almost universal spread of anti-Semitism today, incredible as it may seem, is only the preliminary blast of the storm which is yet to come. There will be a false calm during the first three and one-half years of the Seventieth Week under the treaty with the Roman beast. Then the storm will break in its final fury, so terrible that our Lord has said, "Except those days should be shortened, there should no flesh be saved; but for the elect's sake those days shall be shortened" (Matt. 24:22). The Greek verb does not mean "decrease," as our English term "shorten" might suggest, but rather the idea of *limitation*. In His mercy, God will definitely "limit" the time of this "great tribulation" to exactly 1260 days. To prolong the period would endanger the very existence of the chosen race.

6. *The end of this final seven-year period will bring to its close the entire series of the Seventy Weeks, and therefore usher in the great blessings promised to Israel in Daniel 9:24.*

"Seventy weeks are determined upon thy people and upon thy holy city, to finish the transgression, and to make an end of sins, and to make reconciliation for [or, purge away] iniquity, and to bring in everlasting righteousness, and to seal up the vision and prophecy, and to anoint the most Holy [A.R.V. marg., a most holy place]." In this passage several points should be noted:

First, all these great blessings have to do with a certain people and a certain city — the Jewish people and the city of Jerusalem. It is Jewish trans-

65

gression and sin that is to be brought to an end. No more, after the close of the Seventieth Week, will this people be found in rebellion against their own God and Messiah.

Second, the phrase "to make reconcilation for iniquity" does not here refer to the death of Christ, as some have assumed, but refers to what God will do for Israel on the basis of the death of Christ. As the late Sir Robert Anderson has already pointed out, the sacrifice itself was not the reconciliation, but rather the means by which the reconciliation was made. At His glorious appearing, which will close the Seventieth Week, our Lord on the basis of His sacrifice at Calvary will "reconcile" the chosen people unto Himself.

Third, "to seal up vision and prophecy" is generally taken to mean that prophecy is to be brought to an end by its fulfillment, but there may also be the further idea that the very fountain of prophecy will be sealed because with the Son of God personally on earth His word will go forth *directly*, no longer through the medium of the prophet.

Fourth, "to anoint a most holy place" (A.R.V. margin) is undoubtedly the correct reading and translation. The reference is to the great millennial Temple which will be consecrated as a place of worship and prayer for all nations at the beginning of Messiah's kingdom. During that blessed age, not to Geneva, nor to Rome, will men come to worship the Lord. But there will be a temple of the Lord in *Jerusalem*, and there God will meet with men in a "holy place" sanctified by the personal presence of our Lord Jesus Christ Himself. This will not abrogate the universality of worship ushered in by Calvary (John 4:21-24), as some have objected, but will add to this universality a further glory in the personal presence of the Son of God on earth. To go up to Jerusalem to worship the Lord will no more detract from the present universality and spirituality of worship than the going to a church-building for worship as we do today. Today even modernistic theologians will spend a great deal of time and energy and money to make the trip to Jerusalem for the purpose of seeing the city where His blessed feet once trod. It will be a thousand times more wonderful to go when He Himself is there once more, as we trust He soon will be.

"Even so, come, Lord Jesus."

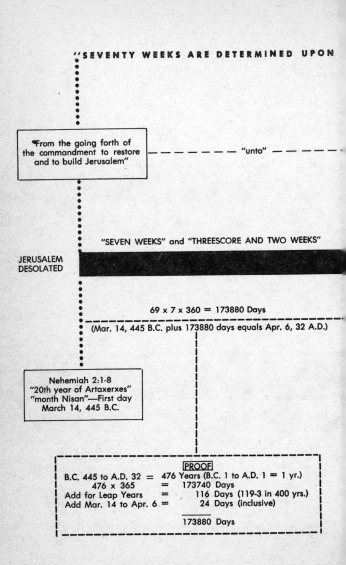

"SEVENTY WEEKS ARE DETERMINED UPON

"From the going forth of the commandment to restore and to build Jerusalem"

"unto"

"SEVEN WEEKS" and "THREESCORE AND TWO WEEKS"

JERUSALEM DESOLATED

69 x 7 x 360 = 173880 Days

(Mar. 14, 445 B.C. plus 173880 days equals Apr. 6, 32 A.D.)

Nehemiah 2:1-8
"20th year of Artaxerxes"
"month Nisan"—First day
March 14, 445 B.C.

PROOF

B.C. 445 to A.D. 32 = 476 Years (B.C. 1 to A.D. 1 = 1 yr.)
476 x 365 = 173740 Days
Add for Leap Years = 116 Days (119-3 in 400 yrs.)
Add Mar. 14 to Apr. 6 = 24 Days (inclusive)

173880 Days

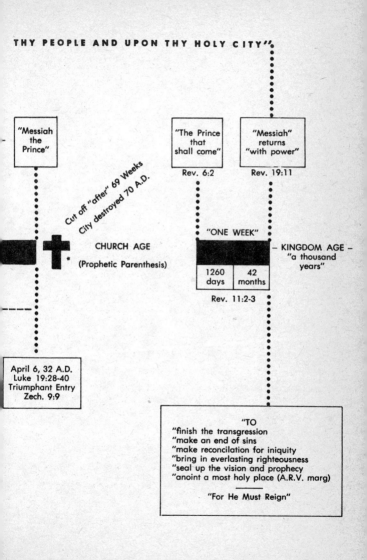

THY PEOPLE AND UPON THY HOLY CITY",

"Messiah
the
Prince"

"The Prince
that
shall come"
Rev. 6:2

"Messiah"
returns
"with power"
Rev. 19:11

Cut off "after" 69 Weeks
City destroyed 70 A.D.

CHURCH AGE
(Prophetic Parenthesis)

"ONE WEEK"

1260
days | 42
months

Rev. 11:2-3

– KINGDOM AGE –
"a thousand
years"

April 6, 32 A.D.
Luke 19:28-40
Triumphant Entry
Zech. 9:9

"TO
"finish the transgression
"make an end of sins
"make reconciliation for iniquity
"bring in everlasting righteousness
"seal up the vision and prophecy
"anoint a most holy place (A.R.V. marg)

"For He Must Reign"

APPENDIX

Note 1. *The Aramaic "Times"* (p. 22)

The Book of Daniel contains a section (2:4 - 7:28) written in the "Syriack" (2:4) or Aramaic language. Although the Aramaic word translated "times" in 7:25 is not dual but plural in form, undoubtedly the plural is here used with a dual significance (see Barnes, Com.; Keil, Com.; also Gesenius, Lex.). This is confirmed by the parallel expression which occurs in Daniel 12:7, "a time, times, and a half," where the word "times" is a dual form in the Hebrew original.

Note 2. *The 360-day Year* (p. 22)

As a practical device, the discrepancy between the lunar year and the solar year was corrected by adding an intercalary thirteenth month approximately every three years; or, more exactly, seven times in nineteen years. However, this somewhat complicated problem does not control the computation of the prophetic year of 360 days as established by Daniel in the Seventy Weeks, and supported by the Apostle John in Revelation 12:13-14.

Note 3. *The Nehemiah Decree* (p. 24)

"This . . . is the only decree which we find recorded in Scripture which relates to the restoring and building of the city" (Tregelles, *Daniel,* page 98).

Note 4. *The Year of Artaxerxes' Accession* (p. 24)

Some readers have been confused by counting the calendar year 465 as the first year of the king's reign, and thus 445 would be the twenty-first year of his reign instead of the twentieth. This apparent discrepancy disappears if we understand that the king's *accession (de jure)* took place in July, 465 B.C., and therefore his first year would actually extend to July, 464. Thus the month Nisan (March) of the king's first year would actually fall in the calendar year 464, and the month Nisan of his twentieth year would fall in the calendar year 445, as stated above. See R. Dick Wilson in the I.S.B.E., article on "Nehemiah."

NOTE 5. *The Chronology of the Gospel Records* (p. 27)

As to the exact chronology of our Lord's life upon earth, there has been wide disagreement even among the most devout scholars. The literature is voluminous and the discordant voices are many. This is particularly the case with reference to the dates of His birth and death. Much of this confusion might be cleared up if proper weight were given to the testimony of the prophet Daniel, and also to that of Luke who was not only a physician but also a competent historian (Luke 1:1-4, 3:1-3). Furthermore, since both wrote by divine inspiration, their testimony should be regarded as decisive.

NOTE 6. *The Present Situation — 1964* (p. 58)

This booklet was first written in 1940, and a great deal has transpired since then. Following World War II, England on May 14, 1948, gave up the Mandate assigned to her under the League of Nations, and moved out of Palestine. On the same date the Jewish authorities — through David Ben Gurion — proclaimed officially the new State of Israel. Without hesitation President Truman, acting for the United States, was the first to give recognition to the new State. The Arab powers at once launched their military attack against Israel, and were decisively defeated. In February of 1949 Israel and Egypt signed an armistice, followed by similar agreements with others of the attacking nations. The State of Israel was accepted into the United Nations organization, and was given recognition by many of its member-nations. However, in spite of all this, the peace now enjoyed by Israel is an uneasy one. Under the

Partition Plan, only about three-fourths of the land of Palestine is now in the hands of the Jewish State. She is still ringed about by implacable Moslem powers which have sworn to destroy Israel and to reoccupy the entire land of Palestine. Israel still desperately needs help.

NOTE 7. *The Revival of the Roman Empire* (p. 60)

Some question has already been raised regarding the revival of the Roman Empire. The curious argument is advanced that since Daniel does not *name* the Roman Empire, therefore it is not included within the scope of his prophecy. This reminds us of the naive Unitarian reasoning that the doctrine of the Trinity is not Biblical because the *word* "Trinity" does not occur in Scripture. Daniel's Prophecy of the Seventy Weeks declares plainly that "the prince that shall come" will arise out of the "people" who would destroy the city of Jerusalem and its Sanctuary (Daniel 9:26). Since everyone who is able to read history knows that this "people" was the Roman Empire, I do not see how Daniel could have identified that Empire more clearly as being in existence at the end time. If we believe in the reality of the "prince that shall come," we shall also have to believe in a Roman Empire out of which he will arise politically. As to this point, we are on solid ground. Just *how* the revival of that Empire will be accomplished is wholly another matter. Here we need to exercise caution in our suggestions. "Prophecy was not given us to enable us to prophesy."